Preface:

Mass media such as press, radio and television, films, play a vital role in socialization, culturalisation and modernization of society. The visual media are bound to have a much greater impact on human mind. But while these media have such a potential value as many educators, they are also susceptible to destructive and harmful uses for promoling criminal, anti – social and selfish escapist tendencies. While their positive potential as mass educators has to be hamessed for developmental purposes, their negative, harmful potential has to be curbed in public interest. Law plays a dual role vis – a vis such media. On the one hand, it protects the creative freedom involved in them, on the other, it has to regulate them so as to avoid their possible abuse.

Indian television has faster and greater impact on society. The National Television network is aimed at fastering social, economic and cultural awareness: promoting the spirit of integration and projecting the progress made by Indians in various fields, Television as an instrument to propagate and inculcate the spirit of nationalism. The Television is a sub-system of culture; a subsystem represents an important variable in the process of social change. It is a huge industry and has thousands of programmes in all the states of India. The small screen has produced numerous celebrities of their own kind some even attaining national fame. TV soaps are extremely popular with housewives as well as working women, literally meaning 'remote view' or 'vicarious view' as the National Television Network of India. The first telecast started on September 15, 1959 in New Delhi.

A SOCIO LEGAL DIMENSION OF TELEVISION IN INDIA

Page No.

Unit – I   Introduction

    1.1   General Introduction

    1.2   Significance of the problem

    1.3   Objectives of the study

    1.4   Hypotheses

    1.5   Methodology

    1.6   Review of Literature

    1.7   Scheme of the study

Unit – II   History, Evolution and Development of Television in India

    2.1   History

    2.2   Evolution

    2.3   Development of television in India

Unit – III   Television Purpose, Uses and Social Impac

       3.1   Purpose and uses of Television

       3.2   Impact on the minds of the people

       3.2.1 Adults

       3.2.2 Children

       3.3.3 Women

       3.3   Socio Economic Impact

Unit – IV   Indian Constitution, other legislations and

Judicial perspective

       4.1   Indian Constitution

       4.2   Judicial perspective

       4.3   Other legislations

Unit – V   Conclusion and suggestions

UNIT-I
INTRODUCTION

1.1 General Introduction

Mass media such as press, radio and television, films, play a vital role in socialization, culturalisation and modernization of society. The visual media are bound to have a much greater impact on human mind. But while these media have such a potential value as many educators, they are also susceptible to destructive and harmful uses for promoling criminal, anti – social and selfish escapist tendencies. While their positive potential as mass educators has to be hamessed for developmental purposes, their negative, harmful potential has to be curbed in public interest. Law plays a dual role vis – a vis such media. On the one hand, it protects the creative freedom involved in them, on the other, it has to regulate them so as to avoid their possible abuse. This paper will deal with such interaction between law and mass media[1].

Television is a form of communication in which still and visual images are transmitted

---

[1] UGC Model Curriculum p. 326

from one point to another through electrical transmission and reception of transient visual images.   The first important discovery occurred in 1875 when Lous May and Willough By smith of England found that, the Electrical conductivity of the element selemium is increased by light. After television is the gradual technical development and is the result of many separate inventions, discoveries and proposals by a large number of scientists.   The Electronic Television invented by Philo. T. Franswarth, in 1927.[2]

The Television in India has been developed gradually and this development is associated with the technological advancement in countries like the United States and Great Britain in this field.   The first centre came to India and was commissioned in Delhi in 1959.   The television became an independent media in 1976.   Prior to that the Television setup was de – linked from All India Radio.   It then proceeded to install transmitters nationwide rapidly for terrestrial broadcasting.   In this period no private enterprise was allowed to set up TV stations or to transmit TV singnals.   Doordarshan introduced Asain Games in 1982, in the eighties when colour

[2] www.television.com

TV was introduced by state owned broadcaster / Doordarshan timed with the 1982 Asian Games which India hosted.[3]

Indian television has faster and greater impact on society. The National Television network is aimed at fastering social, economic and cultural awareness: promoting the spirit of integration and projecting the progress made by Indians in various fields, Television as an instrument to propagate and inculcate the spirit of nationalism. The Television is a sub-system of culture; a subsystem represents an important variable in the process of social change. It is a huge industry and has thousands of programmes in all the states of India. The small screen has produced numerous celebrities of their own kind some even attaining national fame. TV soaps are extremely popular with housewives as well as working women, literally meaning 'remote view' or 'vicarious view' as the National Television Network of India. The first telecast started on September 15, 1959 in New Delhi.

---

[3] www.indiantelevision.com

The central government launched a series of economic and social reforms in 1991 under the period Prime Minister P.V.Narasimha Rao.[4] Under the new policies the government allowed private and foreign broadcasters to engage in limited operations in India. Television serves as a major communication link between groups, collections together the member of different tastes, cultures for common exposure of the dominant culture. It acts as an integrative influence of the society.

The Television as an agent of social change is reinforcing of the value system and it reflects the existing social structure. Television has raised hopes for a higher standard of living. It has become a significant agent to get the information. The influence of Television on social patterns will become stronger as succeeding generating are transmitted a culture through this medium. The extent of television impact on society is yet to be fully documented, and its effects can not be pointed to any specific instance. The question whether television medium is an agent of change or reinforces of status quo cannot be answered in

---

[4] www.indiantelevision.com

a general way. The multitude of studies on the effects of TV on human behavior has restated society carrer with effects. Mass media is viewed as a contributory agent but not the sole cause in the process of reinforcing existing conditions or in bringing out change.

Television has got both positive and negative impact an individuals, family and society. Television with its entertaining and information programmes brought family members together. Its contents provide subject matter to talk, discuss and facilitate greater interaction among the household members. Introduction of television in the household influenced the marital relations. It reduced conversation between married couples. The television also has reduced interaction between family members. Various researches found serial isolation, failure to achieve social integration and lack of social interaction lead to high television viewing. Television viewing can be used to avoid social transaction or can be a shared activity in which members find the opportunity to talk, to sit close or to be quietly companionable.

Television viewing will be stimulus to social interaction. Television is instrumental in keeping family at home in the evening. It is to be considered whether physical presence before television encourages or discourages social interactions. Sex and age variables of the viewers also influence their motivational skills. The freedom of speech and expression includes liberty to propagate not one's views only. It also includes the right to propagate or publish the views of other people; otherwise this freedom would not include the freedom of the press[5].

Freedom of expression has four broad special purposes to serve:
1. It helps an individual, to attain self-fulfillment:
2. It assist in the discovery of truth;
3. It strengthens the capacity of an individual in participating in decision making: and
4. It provides a mechanism by which it would be possible to establish a reasonable balance between stability and social change. All members of society should be

---

[5] Article 19(1) (a) of the Indian constitution

able to form their own beliefs and communicate them freely to others.[6]

The role of the media is vital in generating a democratic culture that extends beyond the political system and becomes engrained in the public consciousness over time. It is through the media that people share their experience, learn and become aware. It is how a constructive political debate about options and policies develops. The media right is exercised in public and therefore has greater effect vis-à-vis what a person says privately. In order for the media to fulfill this function, it must guarantee its objectivity; the journalist should always be a neutral observer, unengaged with events but faithfully recording them. The following information will outline the key requisites necessary for a robust and balanced media industry and highlight some of the issues that are facing working journalists today.

Media could become selective in publishing news and views, for they might have their own interests to serve, especially when it is organized

---

[6] Jain M.P constitutional law of India, Asian law house, Delhi, 2008, pp.187 – 189.

as business. Monopolistic tendencies of the big business houses play a crucial role in the realm of press because of the very fact that press would help them in protecting their interests by disturbing public opinion and/or creating an opinion favorable to them. Even the governments might try to influence press-people covertly by offering favors.

Accuracy is at the heart of the television business. Viewers of 24 hour channels expect speed, but it is the responsibility of TV channels to keep accuracy, and balance, as precedence over speed. If despite this there are errors, channels should be transparent about them. Errors must be corrected promptly and clearly, whether in the use of pictures, a news report, a caption, a graphic or a script. Channels should also strive not to broadcast anything which is obviously defamatory or libelous. Truth will be a defense in all cases where a larger public interest is involves, and in even these cases, equal opportunities will be provided for individuals involved to present their point of view. This also applies in cases where television channels report on those holding public office, though by virtue of doing so, no person can claim immunity from scrutiny from or criticism by channels.

TV channels must provide for neutrality by offering equality for all affected parties, players and actors in any dispute or conflict to present their point of view. Though neutrality does not always come down to giving equal space to all sides' channels must strive to ensure that allegations are not portrayed as fact and charges are not conveyed as an act of guilt.[7]

Television has greater reach, and more immediate impact than other forms of media, and this makes it all the more necessary that channels exercise restraint to ensure that any report or visuals broadcast do not induce, glorify, incite, or positively depict violence and its perpetrators, regardless of ideology or context. Specific care must be taken not to broadcast visuals that can be prejudicial or inflammatory. Equally, in the reporting of violence the act of violence must not be glamorized, because it may have a misleading or desensitizing impact on viewers. Channels will ensure that such reconstructions will not cross

---

[7] www.televisionchennal.com

boundaries of good taste and sensibility. This includes taking adequate precaution while showing any visual instance of pain, fear or suffering, and visual instance of pain, fear or suffering, and visuals or details of methods of suicide and self harm of any kind and will not cross boundaries of good taste and decency.

Channels will ensure that no woman or juvenile, who is a victim of sexual violence, aggression, trauma, or has been a witness to the same is shown on television without due effort taken to conceal the identity. In reporting all cases of sexual assault, or instances where the personal character or privacy of women is concerned, their names, pictures and other details will not be telecasted. Similarly, the identity of victims of child abuse and juvenile delinquents will not be revealed, and their pictures will be morphed to conceal their identity.

Channels will ensure that they do not show, without morphing, nudity of the male or female form. Channels will also not show explicit images of sexual activity or sexual perversions or acts of sexual violence like rape or molestation, or show pornography, or the use of sexually suggestive language.

The nation is today passing through a terrible socio-economic crisis. Artists, Writers and media persons must start acting responsibly and help the people who are suffering terribly in solving their problems. And this they can do by focusing on the real issues which are basically economic and not by trying to divert the attention of the people. The committee of the press council of India has formed guidelines to require a revolutionary change in the media projection of women with much more punch added to it. The media both electronic and print media are normally and legally bound to avoid identification of victims of sex crimes. Section 228 A of Indian Penal Code and press council guidelines 1 to 6 are very explicit in this regard. The committee also laid guidelines to slide in normal ethos to be checked by combating obscenity and vulgarity. For this the press council supports a policy of self regulation as any form of censorship anathema to the rights and the guarantees enshrined in our constitution. A high level interaction between NGO's in moulding and creating public opinion disfavoring vulgarity and obscenity.

The Official Secrets Act. 1923 (Act XIX of 1923) has been passed to consolidate and amend the law relating to official secrets. The act is aimed at maintaining security of the state against leakage of secret information, sabotage and like. It deals with two kinds of offences, namely Spying[8] and wrongful communication[9] of secret information. Sec 5 of the act gives the executive power to prosecute any one disclosing official information, or any person voluntarily receiving such information[10].

The young persons (Harmful publications) Act, 1956 aim is prohibiting the production in India of crime and violent telecast. Harmful publications are dealt within section 2 of the Act. It means any book, magazine, pamphlet, news paper or other publication which consist of stories with the aid of picture or without the aid of pictures or wholly in pictures being stories portraying wholly or mainly (1) The commission

---

[8] Section 3 of the Official Secrets Act. 1923.
[9] Section 5 of the Official Secrets Act. 1923.
[10] Section 5 (2) of the Official Secrets Act. 1923.

of offences or (ii) Acts of violence or cruelty or (iii) Incidents of repulsive or horrible nature.

Media freedom is fundamental for free public discussion, education and to the life of an individual in a democratic polity. The media is one of the vital pillars of a free society. The right to freedom of speech and expression[11] extends to communication media sections. Electronic media have emerged as major factors in the nation's life. The electronic media is still expanding and in the process becoming more inquisitive.

Clause (2) of Article 19 contains the grounds on which restrictions on the freedom of speech and expression can be imposed.

(a) Security of the State, (b) Friendly Relations with foreign States. (c) Public Order (d) Decency of Morality. (e) Contempt of Court. (f) Defamation. (g) Incitement of an offence. (h) Sovereignty and integrity of India[12].

---

[11] Article 19 (1) (a) of the Indian Constitution.
[12] Pandey J.N Constitutional Law of India, Central Law agency year 2007. p. 191.

The main thrust of the study to find out the effects of television watching by people and its sociologic consequences. The impact of television watching was seen with regard to violence, sex, crudity, depicted in television shows and its diverse impact on people. Attempts were also made to find out the extent to which exposure to satellite television programmes has created a change in the cultural, social and ethical values. The awareness of legal consequences among the viewers also been solicited. The historical background of the advent of television and its consequential growth is being observed. The freedom of the press: Whether it can be extendable to television and the constitutional and legislative procedure is presented for a clear understanding of the study.

1.2 Significance of the Problem :

The researcher selected this problem to analyze and evaluate the information regarding the mass media with regard to socio – legal dimensions of television and advantages and disadvantages of television. The television is considered to be a part of a process called the social construction of reality. People use to gain knowledge from the television and to form an image of the world and behave in accordance with the perceived reality of that image. The media is felt to be especially important in the social construction.

There is a direct relationship between Television and Society. By this, concern was shown a legal regulation of mass media. The present study is primarily focused on the impact of television on the people and children specifically. The laws enacted by the legislature and judicial perspective are also addressed in the present study. The television changed the society, perceptions, of violence, crime and criminal justice. Today the parental authority is being graded and tomorrow it may turn of the society. Influed by the violence in media young children are resorting to crimes the nature of which crosses the imagination also such under influence has been the concern of this study, to know about its extent and to assess the influence it yield. Hence the researcher has selected this problem / topic for study.

1.3 Objective of the Study :

The following are the major objectives

1. To study the genesis, growth, advantages and disadvantages of television is India.
2. To evaluate the role played by the mass media and law.
3. To study the impact of Television on children and women.
4. To evaluate the information relating to legal and constitutional aspects of television.
5. To find out the role of judiciary.

1.4 Methodology :

Basing on the nature of the topic the researcher has followed secondary method of study and collected the relevant data from the various vertical and horizontal sources like law books, journals, periodicals website through internet and other related interdisciplinary sources. The study also covers historical, analytical and comparative methods. The collected data was analyzed and placed in the appropriate units.

1.5 Hypotheses :

The following hypotheses are formulated to carry out the research effectively and meaningfully.

- Visual media like Television more effective in importing information and influencing people.
- The addiction of Television leads to loss of social and human relations.

1.6 Review of literature

Literature in connection with the present problem is reviewed from the earlier studies where in published books are the main source. Dorr Annie, in his book Television and Children a special medium for special audience (2006) Covers the impact of television on children the depictions of violence crudity, obscenity and their impact on children.

Gopal Saxena in his book Television in India (2005), covered changes and challenges of the impact of television on society.

Jain M.P in his book entitled constitutional law of India (2007), critically determined the various aspects relating to right to freedom of press it include media.

Varadarajulu K. in his Dissertation entitled Mass media regulation influence of television on children, Covered geneses and growth of television system in India and highlighted the influence of television on children.

The researcher collected data by exploring internet websites like www.indiantelevision.com/ Indian broadcast/history/of ------. It provides history of the television and mass media law.

www.wikipedia.org/wiki/Television-in-india gives a brief understanding of the television is India which led for the development of the country.

www.indianchild .com/ India – television -----deals with TV channels in India television.

www.Documents and setting / sarada / Desktop / psychological impact of television serials. 3/2/2009. It provides basic information of the TV serials in India.

Markandy Raju, in his article, the role of art, literature and the media. All India reporter, 2009 focused on historical improvements of the mass media.

1.7 Scheme of the study :

The researcher has designed the research work to carry out the objects of the study easily and effectively. After selecting the research problem, the researcher has extensively studied the literature and through scanning of the material the researcher organized all material in an orderly manner.

The entire study is divided into five Unit dealing with different aspects of the problem. First Unit covers the introduction consisting of significance of the problem including objectives of the study, methodology followed. Hypotheses formulated, literature reviewed and scheme of the study.

The second Unit is History, evolution and development of television in India which deals with the history and growth of the television.

The third Unit is Television: purpose uses and social impact. It covered the present impact of television on adult, children and women in the society.

The fourth Unit is Indian constitution, other legislations and judicial perspective, which deals with Mass media and law.

The Fifth Unit is concluding unit contains the findings and based on the study and certain constructive suggestions.

UNIT-II

History, Evolution and Development of Television in India

2.1 History

Television is a form of communication in which still and visual images are transmitted from one point to another through electrical transmission and reception of transient visual images. Like motion pictures, television consists of a series of successive images, which are registered on the brain as a continuous picture due to the persistence of vision. The word means, "Vision at a distance". Each visual image impressed on the eye persists for a fraction of a second.

Television is the gradual technical development and is the result of many separate inventions, discoveries and proposals by a large number of scientists. The telegraph and telephone

---

[13] McGrawhill Encyclopedia of Science and Tech., 1993, pp,56-58,Vol.13 ,

had extended communication by signals for words. The first important discovery occurred in 1873[13] when Lous May and Willoughby Smith of England found that the electrical conductivity of the element selenium is increased by light.

This discovery has led to various attempts in 1875 by G.R. Gary, in 1897 by Karl F. Brawn. They designed a television system and introduced the cathode-ray tube respectively. The gradual development of radio is a means of providing sound of television and as a method of transmitting the pictures.

In America experimental television transmission began in General Electric laboratory and the G.E. presented the first American dramatic production on television on September 11, 1928. The British Broadcasting Corporation began its regular television broadcasts in the year 1936 in Great Britain. The NBC in America began its regular service in 1939 starting off with the opening ceremonies at the New York World's fair.

The Federal Communication Commission (FCC) began in the United States with television broadcasters and set manufacturers accepting uniform standards and hearing by the FCC. This process started during 1935[14]. The FCC authorized commercial televisions beganon July 1, 1941 in New York. The FCC with its Sixth Report and Order lifted several restrictions in April 1952. The FCC approved colour television systems developed by CBS in 1951, but it was abandoned shortly.

The use, of colour televisions in American began with the FCC issuing rules for these frilly electronic, compatible systems by National Television Systems Committee (NTSC) in January 1953. This system is in use in the United States ever since.

The Educational Television Facilities Act of 1962, in the United States provided federal aid to educational television. This important legislative Act has resulted in many new ETV establishments, in 1965 the Carhergie Commission was formed to study ETV and make recommendations regarding its future. The report of the commission was issued in 1967 and formed the basis of the Public Broadcasting Act passed in the same year. The Public Broadcasting Act

---

[14] Encyclopedia Americana, The Encyclopedia Britanica, New standard Encyclopaedia,1992,pp 32-35

redirected ETC from its original educational purpose to that of serving as an alternative to commercial television by offering an indeed range programmes.

The local commercial broadcasting faced criticism as the local stations had abdicated its responsibility to serve community needs and in return for guaranteed, risk free profits has "sold" themselves for the net work. The FCC proposed a rule-limiting network programming in the top 50 markets to three hours of prime time in 1971.

The biggest change in television broadcasting in the emergence of cable television. The FCC initially had no jurisdiction over them under the communication Act of 1934. In 1966 the FCC asserted its jurisdiction over all cable TV systems and adopted rules. The new FCC rules in 1972 and others later in the decade significantly contributed to the growth of cable television.

The American Television industry throughout its developmental stages was governed by the communications Act of 1934. He set up the federal communications commission as an independent regulatory agency. The commission consisted of seven members, each appointed for a 7-year term. The commission maintains a degree of control by issuing licenses and through regulation.

The FCC does not censor programmes nor can it control the form or content of programmes. It has no control of the quality of television. The commission may insist on fairness in dealing with issues of public concern, and it has the power to refuse to reserve license in the public interest.

2.2 Evolution

Television transmission got a cue from America in various countries in developing their own networks. By 1970's more than 100 countries had television. Countries like Britain, USSR, West Germany, Japan had more than 100 stations where as India has one or two stations and fewer than 10,000 TV receivers.

The television in India has developed gradually. This development is associated with the technological advancement in countries like the United States and Great Britain in this field. The first television centre was commissioned in

Delhi on an experimental basis in 1959. The transmission was started with a grant of UNESCO. The range of the transmitter was forty kilometers.

The television set up was de-linked from All India Radio during 1976 The television became an independent media in the Ministry of Information and Broadcasting under the new banner — "DOORDARSHAN" In January 1976 television introduced commercial services The Government started entertainment programmes along with informational programmes Through commercial transmission sports and Sponsored Programmes started.[15]

\

In 1975, the satellite instructional television experiment was started. This was intended to disseminate information on various subjects. The programmes covered subjects like agriculture, health, hygiene, family and child welfare, and adult education. The programmes covered 2,400 villages in Andhra Pradesh, Bihar, Karnataka, Orissa, Rajasthan, Madhya Pradesh and Gujarat.

---

[15] www.Indiantelevision.com

The programmes were transmitted through satellites for one year.

The year 1982 was a major landmark in the Indian television history when colour television was introduced. In the same year INSTAT −1A, the indigenous communication satellites was launched. This was the first generation satellite meant for communication. Live telecast, microwave system was also introduced in the same year with which the number of television users and viewers was remarkably increased. The reach of television signals in the country also predominantly increased.

The television in India was introduced 25 years after its invention and 30 years after its inception. This communication process appears to be in a formation stage as a medium of communication. In 30th August 1983, 1NSAT 1 B was launched. In February 1987, morning transmission was started and from 26th January 1989 afternoon transmission was introduced for the housewives. The Doordarshan was separated from the All India Radio on April 1976. Operate within the parameters of the Ministry of Information and Broadcasting.

The report of the working group of Autonomy for Akshavani and Doordarshan better known as Verghes Committee Report identified seven factors for autonomy Report identified seven factors for autonomy they are Substance not form

1. The question of autonomy is not a matter of its nomenclature, but the real substance that matters

2. Monopoly evokes restraint Autonomy for broadcast media in inconceivable in monopolistic system.

3. Not a gift Autonomy on its own does not come nor is given so easily. It has to be earned by consistent and systematic efforts.

4. Culture of Independence: The concept of autonomy concerns the management of the organisation.

5. Objective measure, accountability: The concept of autonomy is not that absolute.

6. Absolute autonomy not possible: The prevalent mode of national planning may not provide absolute autonomy.

7. The national environment: The environment moulds the tact and working of autonomy.

The Bhagavantam' s Committee in 1965 and the Chanda Committee in 1966 had recommended autonomous corporation for television and Radio. During the emergency days the government's attitude towards and radio and television became stiffer. The Joshi committee that submitted its report to the government in 1984 on the issue of Software policy for Doordarshan was of the opinion that Indian Television's present structure hampers creativity. The TV has to act as an agent of development communication and it has to work towards national confidence building:

Without autonomy the creating media like radio and television would arrange in red-tapism and would not some the desired purpose. In building a New Work Information and Communication order, the role of television cannot be over emphasized[16].

Television occupies a very prominent place in the ongoing communication revolution in

---

[16] www.Indiantelevisionhistory.com

India. It has the potential to play the role of a catalyst of social change by doing the following:

1. Disseminating information;
2. Educating the masses;
3. Human resource development;
4. Helping in the process of development communication;
5. Inculcation of scientific temper among people;
6. Providing meaningful entertainment;
7. National integration;
8. Promotion of culture;
9. Promotion of debates and discussion on public issues; and
10. Motivation

These potentials can be utilised only if a sound television policy based on a genuinely Indian perspective is formulated and implemented.

2.3 Development of Television in India

The Doordarshan is providing the national channel through power transmitters. The DD-2 and sports channel and the regional language channels are telecast through satellite. In Great Britain the British Broadcasting Corporation Operates two channels BBC −1 and BBC −2.

This kind of television is usually supported by annual taxes. In European and third World Countries the revenue is augmented by income from advertisers. In government controlled television commercials are restricted as to content and are limited to a certain number and to certain times of the day. In authoritarian regimes the television is highly regiment, and propagandistic, even the entertainment shows often reflect official government positions. The commercial television provides a variety of entertainment shows, news and other programmes. These are operated for profit and this kind of television is developing recently. Countries, which have government, controlled stations also permit the operation of commercial stations. These stations sell their broadcast time and make its facilities available to advertisers. They in term either sponsor or buy time for spot announcements.

These television stations present programmes appeal to the public in order to attract viewers. Programmes are rated on the basis of a rating system, which measure the percentage of viewing audience held by each programme in its time period. The criticism on commercial stations is that of the quality of programmes and the importance attached to ratings. Increased government regulation, as a means to force commercial television stations to devote more time to the interest of smaller audience is necessary. It is argued that such measures are contrary to the principles of free enterprise and constitute a threat of freedom of speech or of the arks.

As an alternative to commercial television public television is designed. It provides cultural and informational material and offers entertainments programmes with special rather than mass appeal. Many public televisions broadcast educational television programmes. State agencies, local school districts, non-profit corporations or universities or colleges own most public television stations.

In America, the Corporation for Public Broadcasting (CPB) is a non-profit corporation established by the Public Broadcasting Act of 1967. In India, though there are no separate Public television channels, the University Grants Commission, NCERT, and all the Universities affiliated to the UGC and state educational institutions produced programmes of educational value. They are transmitted through Doordarshan[17].

The United States has three systems of pay television Cable television, subscription over — the — air — television, and multiunit distribution service. In cable television the transmission takes place through satellite. The signals are received through dish antennas and disseminated to the viewers and through cable network. Cable customers receive programming through a local cable company, which provides programme material from a variety of sources. Cable service provides the customer with access to a fixed member of channels for a monthly rental fee. Additional channels, called pen cable channels are available for an additional fee.

Pay-cable networks, whose material is available only on Pay-Cable channels, provide programmes without commercial interruption. They show first run movies and telecasts of entertainment specials and sports events. Their movies, unlike most of these shown on over-the-air television are indecent. The largest pay cable networks are Home Box Office, Movie hannel.

---

[17] www.Doordarshantelecastcom

The total family viewing of these channels is a question for considerable debate in view of their quality[18].

---

[18] Encyclopedia Americana, The Encyclopedia Britanica, New standard Encyclopedia, 1992, pp32-35

UNIT- III
Television purpose, uses and social impact

3.1 Purpose and uses of Television

Media are considered as an agent of social change. The media are believed to be active in bringing about changes in the attitudes or behaviours of the mass audience. Television serves as a major communication link between groups, collections together the members of different tastes, cultures for common exposure of the dominant culture. It acts as an integrative influence in the society.

Mc Cannock[19] opines that mass media information plays a peculiar teacher's role, that of a 'history-teacher'. Mass communication information is no mirror but mould of opinions and attitudes in the population. The free and adequate plan of information could serve to widen horizons, enlist support for social change.

The television as an agent of social change is a reinforce of the value system and it reflects

---

[19] www.massmediainformation.com

the existing social structure. Television contents are value free and they avoid those issues, which are controversial and might provoke change.

Television has raised hopes for a higher standard of living. It has become a significant agent in the rearing of children. It has profoundly affected the process of socialization. The influence of television on social patterns will become stronger as succeeding generations are transmitted a culture through this medium. The extent of television impact on society is yet to be frilly documented, and its effects cannot be pointed to any specific instance.

The question whether television medium is an agent of change or reinforces of status quo cannot be answered in a general way. The multitude of studies on the effects of TV on human behaviour has restated society career with effects. Mass media is viewed as a contributory agent but not the sole cause in the process of reinforcing existing conditions or in bringing about change. Media does influence individual does not so among and through a nexus of mediator factors and influences.

3.2 Impact on the minds of the people

Television viewing is serving as a catalyst of change. It offers an opportunity for parents to explore with youngsters the social and emotional aspects of various human experiences. It offers the parents new insights into personalities of their children. Television watching reduces boredom and loneliness. It is not treated as an individual activity but a family activity as in India television viewing is a family affair.

Television with its entertaining and informative programmes brought family members together. Its contents provide subject matter to talk, discuss and facilitate greater interaction among the household members. Introduction of television in the household influenced the marital relations. It reduced conversation between married couples. The television also has reduced interaction between family members. Various researches found serial isolation, failure to achieve social integration and lack of social interaction leads to high television viewing.

Television viewing can be used to avoid social interaction or can be a shared activity in which members find the opportunity to talk, to sit close or to be quietly companionable. Television viewing will be stimulus to social interaction. There is a two-way relation between mass media and family. The television medium is likely to affect internal dynamics. It can also influence familial social and cultural ethos. The family undergoes many changes once it acquires a television set. Television is instrumental in keeping family at home in the evening. It is to be considered whether physical presence before television encourages or discourage social interactions. Sex and age variables of the viewers also influence their motivational skills.

A threat to cultural ethos of India is posed by mass media. Both indigenous and foreign media invaded our cultural traditions. There is every danger of succumbing to an imitative culture and losing its indigenous creative genius. The parliamentary standing committee on Human Resource Development[20] evolved a creative response to this new challenge, which

---

[20] In its twelfth report in 1994

will enable us to presence our cultural continuity with the past. It rejected the blameful and integrating the desirable in the influences, which are entering our country through the new electronic technology. The committee recommended that the NPC should explore measures to make the mass media an effective instrument for the dissemination of culture. It expressed serious concern over the ever increasing and reckless exhibition of violence, anti social activities and obscenity, the worst sufferers of which are the younger generation whose finer sensibilities are being coarsened and creative facilities dulled.

Television with its rapid rise to prominence among entertainment media is in the focus as violence in the mass media has been subject of continuing controversy. Television's depiction of violence rate at least fifty times greater than in real life and with children's programming far exceeding general audience programme in violent episodes. Effects of media violence and its influence on social behaviour are a much debatable controversies. The average American child in growing form a 5 year old to 4 year old would witness the violent deaths of 13,000 human beings on television, but it has been difficult to drawn definite conclusions from such statistics. A national survey in America in 1968 by Louis Harris pollsters for the National Commission on the causes and prevention of violence showed that 59% of male adults and 63% of female adults felt there was too much violence. 52 percent felt it likely that television triggered violent acts from persons who are socially maladjusted or mentally unstable and 32 percent of the population felt it likely that television makes people insensitive to actual acts of violence.

It is a demonstrated principle of psychology that desensitized and habituated responses will approach and often return to their initial levels when the stimuli are removed for a period. Continuous exposure to shows featuring extreme violence against women increases the acceptance of "rape-myth". The evidence of several experiments that used children as subjects suggest that violence in the media deadens response to media violence.

The Working Group on Doordarshan software in its report in April 1982 made it clear that "the objection is to vulgarity, and not to so call permissiveness, which has always existed". No organization whether publicly or privately owned should be allowed to broadcast such material via transmitter or cable, for reception inside homes. The objectives underlying legislation such as the Cinematograph Act and the Indecent Representation of Women (Prohibition) Act are being violated and Doordarshan and cable operators are permitted by the Government to disseminate foreign channel telecasts of programmes that are grossly offensive to decency and good taste.

The television is often viewed by three generations of a family. To watch a lewd or sadistic film scene in a family group is highly embarrassing. In a seminar on 'Film for Television"[21]. Adoor Gopalakrishnan regretted that with the expansion of the television network in the country vulgarity would be more widely disseminated. The seminar evolved the need to learn from the experience of other countries where the depiction of unbridled violence and sex on television had promoted crime. There have

---

[21] organized by the Indian Institute of Mass Communication in January, 1983

been signs of citizen awareness and protect, alongside citizen acquiescence. The press has rendered a public service by conveying the distress and disgust of their readers and publishing news of the consequences of violence depicted on the television. The Indian Express reported on 23 August 1995- TV serial leads to suicide "Bangalore - Apparently influenced by a suicide scene in a television serial, Nandeesh, a teenager, hanged himself to death at his residence here on Sunday, the police said. A student of St.Joseph's high school, Nandeesh had been experimenting daredevil acts shown on TV and was in the habit of emulating such acts.

The competition among the satellite channels has made the picture worst. With a view to keep its audience base in control they are resorting to unethical practices. To uphold the competition same channels started masala mix programmes, sex, violence, obscenity is being telecast without any hindrance. The Cable Television Regulation Act framed guidelines for cable networks operating in the country. This Act has not effect on the cable television industry, which often overrides the norms of censor and telecast objectionable programmes. Even the advertisers are not following the advertising code. Obscene shots are being telecast in middle of any programme irrespective of the audience group to which such programmes are aimed.

The time theory plays an important role in the control of miscarriage of television programmes. When children are already off the television set late in the night it is suggested that late night-films should be telecast at late night hours. On the basis of a series of experiments, depictions of sexual violence rather than of explicit Sex per se appear to affect attitudes the Most[22] Anti social effects arise either from exposure to violent pornography or from materials that are sexually violent but not sexually explicit[23] depictions of sexual violence foster antisocial attitudes about women and rape. Television has been more related to fear of crime. It being more visual and emotional in content would naturally tend to affect emotional attitudes such as fear and concern. The relationship between the media and beliefs and attitudes about crime ultimately depends on three factors:

---

[22] Imrich et a)., 1990; Linz 1989

[23] Ibid

45

The medium being discussed; the medium's style of presentation and crime and justice content; and the experiences, predisposition, and immediate community of the consumer[24]

It can be observed that whether the media influence the formation of public policies with regard to crime and justice and the support received by specific policies. Effects in this area are considered the most important of the three types of effects namely agenda setting, attitudes and beliefs, and policies.

News media significantly affect policy preferences for general social issues. Pandian[25] asserted that "Television viewing elicits irrational policy support, heavily tilted toward a law and order punitive orientation". Even students who achieved high grades, are heavy readers, and are aware that television content is "meal" come to devalue due process consideration such as protection of civil liberates. And even among those already holding mainstream views, heavy

---

[24] Surette, R. 1992

[25] 1978, p.455

crime show viewing promotes conventionality and heightened support for increased social control[26].

The media must be viewed as both messengers and actions in the criminal justice policy arena. The highly idiosyncratic and interactive nature of the relationship between the media the decision making process with regard to criminal justice policy, the effects of the media cannot yet be predicted with confidence at the individual level. It is a demonstrated principle of psychology that desensitized and habituated responses will approach and often return to their initial levels when the stimuli are removed for a period. Continuous exposure to shows featuring extreme violence against women increases the acceptance of "rape-myth". The evidence of several experiments that used children as subjects suggest that violence in the media deadens response to media.

The Working Group on Doordarshan software in its report in April 1982 made it clear that "the objection is to vulgarity, and not to so

---

[26] Carlson, 1985,p. 189

call permissiveness, which has always existed". No organization whether publicly or privately owned should be allowed to broadcast such material via transmitter or cable, for reception inside homes. The objectives underlying the legislation such as the Cinematograph Act[27] and the Indecent Representation of Women (Prohibition) Act[28] are being violated and Doordarshan and cable operators are permitted by the Government to disseminate foreign channel telecasts of programmes that are grossly offensive to decency and good taste.

The television is often viewed by three generations of a family. To watch a lewd or sadistic film scene in a family group is highly embarrassing. There have been signs of citizen awareness and protect, alongside citizen acquiescence. The press has rendered a public service by conveying the distress and disgust of their readers and publishing news of the consequences of violence depicted on the television. The Indian Express reported on 23 August 1995- TV serial leads to suicide "Bangalore - Apparently influenced by a suicide

---

[27] 1918
[28] 1986

scene in a television serial, Nandeesh, a teenager, hanged himself to death at his residence here on Sunday, the police said. A student of St.Joseph's high school, Nandeesh had been experimenting daredevil acts shown on TV and was in the habit of emulating such acts.

The ides and values in the society keep on changing, suiting the call and clime of lime. This applies to mass communication also. Not only ideals, but also the manner and method of communication must change. These basic principles of communication are equally relevant to television. Public response and social objectives cannot always go together, especially in case of mass media. New urges and aspirations of people have to be respected and responded.

The broadcasting media has to conform to the 'code' and traditions and at the same time cannot shy away from arousing in people a curiosity for knowledge. Sex has been one of the most baffling and bewildering enigmas in India. It is considered to be a strictly personal and private affair. There are people who feel that to talk about sex with children around would have dangerous repercussions on their minds and morals. The concept of 'sublimation of sex', as profounded by (Freud) and others suggests that the sexual impulse in man is easily transformable into higher mental activities such as charity, love of art, interest in science etc., There is no need to be too realistic in projecting sex, even if it forms an integral part of a story. It might shock our children and youth. It has to be gradually introduced to the family-audience that television has. Crudity and vulgarity in the name of sex would be harmful for the adolescent.

The television audience is entirely different in composition and character from those of commercial feature films and cheap magazines. Television can afford to portray sex with its beautiful manifestations. Sex is a social responsibility. Sex in a play should deal with in a subtle and suggestive manner.

There is not much of a difference in the projection of crudity, vulgarity and exposure in Doordarshan or in any private owned channel. Needless to say, every person so inclined should have the freedom to view films portraying sex in the raw or sadistic violence on his own video equipment or he is free to read pornographic literature in privacy. No organization publicly or privately owned should be allowed to broadcast such material, for public viewing.

The members of the consultative Committee of Parliament attached to the Ministry of Information and Broadcasting in its meeting held on May 13 1994 wanted "aping of alien values" eschewed in Indian television. The same report was published[29] quoted Sunil Dutt, M.P., saying that 'in the good old days there was not much of violence and vulgarity shown in films as is being done now". Vijayanthimala Bali during her prime days she had never indecently exposed. The Minister for Information and Broadcasting, K.P.Singh Deo assured the Committee that corrective measures would be initiated soon. There will be no compromise, on the efforts to rid Indian films of sex, violence and vulgarity", he observed. He also added "Doordarshan has taken the step not to telecast songs and dance numbers that are not cleared by the Censor Board".

The feature films and film-based programmes have always been on the top of the

---

[29] In The Times of India, dated July 17 1994

popularity chart. Film shows continue to be among the highest rates ones. Their number has also increased. The choice of songs, and dance sequences for such programmes reflect a very poor taste. The vulgarity and obscenity in them seem to have crossed the limits of decency. The unabashed flashing of skirts, the hero pulling up the sari of heroine while other dancing girls raising in the background raising their saris by themselves is not for family viewing either. There have been protests in Parliament; even the Prime Minister expressed his anguish over the ever-increasing crudity and exposure of sex in the film shows on television. This certainly is not entertainment that Indian viewers would accept and appreciate for long.

3.2.1 Adults

Watching television in childhood and adolescence has been linked to adverse health indicators including obesity, poor fitness, smoking, and raised cholesterol. However, there have been no longitudinal studies of childhood viewing and adult health. We explored these associations in a birth cohort followed up to age 26 year.

Average weeknight viewing between ages 5 and 15 years was associated with higher body-mass indices, lower cardio respiratory fitness, increased cigarette smoking, and raised serum cholesterol. Childhood and adolescent viewing had no significant association with blood pressure. These associations persisted after adjustment for potential confounding factors such as childhood socioeconomic status, body-mass index at age 5 years, parental body-mass index, parental smoking, and physical activity at age 15 years. In 26-ycar-olds, population - attribute fractions indicate that 17% of overweight, 15% of raised serum cholesterol, 17% of smoking, and 15% of poor fitness can be attributed to watching television for more than 2 hours a day during childhood and adolescence[30]. Television viewing in childhood and adolescence is associated with overweight, poor fitness, smoking, and raised cholesterol in adulthood. Excessive viewing might have long-lasting adverse effects on health.

---

[30] www.televisioninfluenceonadults.com

3.2.2 Children

Children do not have the skills and life experience of adults and this makes them vulnerable to television content. From the earliest days of the medium adults have express concern about television's influence on childrens. Parents have shown anxiety about the influence of violence on TV programmes and have worried about the effects of television on the taste of their children. Plato's 'Republic' urged careful control of ideas and stories presented to children.

Information, education and entertainment are often stated to be the objectives of the mass media. But studies show that the direct contribution of television to children's education is minimal. Its contribution to enrichment of general knowledge is high. Children also study less on account of pre-occupation with television. Television had a negative impact on studies below 15 years of children.

Television also is a carrier of polluting influences. With the advent of television children wanted to buy everything advertised on television. It leaves little to imagination. Before television came, radio was a much better medium. As radio did not provide visuals, this has resulted in picturisation mentally what was referred to. This helped to improve the imaginative power of listeners. Now, this power is totally lost.

A round table discussion was organized by C.M.S. in Delhi on the theme of vulgarity and violence in Mass Media on 22nd September 1994. In this discussion Justice Ranganatha Mishra observed that children tend to imitate in their actions what they see being done by adults. This point was illustrated by several participants who cited the finding of research, conducted in India and abroad, establishing a direct link between juvenile crime and the depiction of violence in media.

Films depicted not only women in an objectionable way but men too. They were presented as villains, rapists, alcoholics, and singers of bawdy songs. Child viewers were exposed along with adults to scenes of murder and rape. Copycat violence and impulsive behaviour was promoted by the exposure of children to scenes of sadism, pelvic thrust and frenzied gyrations in the name of dance[1].

The exhibition of vulgarity should be treated as a crime. In connection with the effect of violence shown on television, the seminar cited a study conducted in West Bengal[31], which showed that 90% of juvenile crime went unreported[32].

The wanton or willful presentation of a person or situation intended to titillate the viewer or listener is defined as obscenity and a scene, which one would not like to share with his or her children might be described as obscene.

Children are a special audience group for television transmission. Television as a medium of communication acquaint the children about different things like family, play group, teacher etc., Its programmes not only educate and entertain the children but also inform and reinforce social values and norms.

Television is treated as a medium through which people learn many things. Television when used for educational purposed has proved to be an excellent aid for learning not only at

---

[31] Nandini Prasad, communication specialist

[32] Manorama Jafa, of the Children's Book Trust

classrooms but also at home. Social learning theory has been the most interested in developing a model of the processes by which television contents influence child behaviour.

Television plays four roles in children's lives-one are that of time consuming activity. Second is that of a social event-an opportunity to snuggle with parents or to escape from quarrelsome children. Third is that of informative processing task. Fourth and final roll is that of information-a source of knowledge. The viewing patters change with age but also differ in different social classes. Television is treated as a powerful source of information to the children who learn a number of things from different programmes. In Indian society, it is the parents who determine the style of life, friendship circle of the children. Television as a source of knowledge and its contents are censored and controlled by parents. Parents are likely to control and regulate the children's television viewing behaviour pattern. This has resulted in both positive and negative consequences for the children. The television viewing helps in seeking knowledge regarding different things and on the other hand, it inhibits the children's imaginative abilities. Under television viewing behaviour pattern the time children spend on television viewing whether television view to change their behaviour are to be taken in to consideration. The motivation for children's to watch television programmes is also another important factor in determining the influence. The role of parents in motivating the children to watch television programmes or to inhibit their television viewing of certain programmes is also a main concern.

With the advent of satellite and direct to home television, this medium has ushered in information revolution. Children are now better equipped with knowledge regarding different places of the world. They have come to know about different styles of life and have learned to develop greater tolerance towards people of other faiths.

Things, which they could not understand and remember after reading books, could now be easily comprehended through television. Television as a medium through which children can learn many new things and it is an important source of information and learning. The children of the lower class who used to loiter around indulged into different mischief and quarrels can spend their time effectively. It also facilitates controlling truancy of children who use to movies escaping classes.

The negative impact of television viewing is that it can adversely affect their studies. The exposure to commercials makes them more demanding. The children can become more obstinate. Television has introduced the children into an adult's world resulting into disappearance of their childhood. The children are exposed to television matured earlier than their age, which would have bad consequences for their future life. With the advent of television into the drawing room children have stopped a number of outdoor activities like play interaction with others. There are complaints also that television watching adversely affected the eyesight. The negative impact of television viewing varies according to class. The lower and middle class generally are concerned about the studies. The upper and middle class feel that television watching can adversely affect the imaginative and creative abilities.

The Payne Fund studies[33], addressed questions about the impact of motion picture content on children's moral beliefs and attitudes. Studies reveal beliefs and attitudes. Studies reveal that changes in physiological measures of emotional response[34] varied with the action portrayed on screen. They documented enormous amounts of children's learning from motion pictures and demonstrated that specific programmes could change children's beliefs about war, crime and punishment and various racial, ethnic and national groups.

Television programmes can encourage variety of positive behaviour. Children ranging from pre-school through high school age understand and learn from pre-social television content. They learn more when the messages are explicitly designed to promote positive behaviour and values, particularly when the portrayals are interesting enough to attract attention and concrete enough to be comprehensible. The classroom setting tends to facilitate such positive outcomes especially when viewing is combined with supplementary activities endemic to the classroom.

---

[33] The Payne Fund studies, 1984
[34] e.g., heart and breathing rate, galvanic skin response

Advances in media technology have improved the surveillance capabilities of law enforcement agencies over the part decade. Programmes designed to reduce victimization and those designed for deterrence both uses the existing mass media distribution system to market anticrime information. The media have been utilized in two ways in the form of traditional advertising and entertainment, and in anticrime programmes that directly incorporate the media's electronic and visual technology.

Entertainment: Style pro-social media efforts initially targeted children, with the basic goal being to counteract the pervasive violent content of the entertainment media. Most research on pro-social media applications has involved children's television programmes. The PBS show[35] in America" Mr.Roger's Neighborhood" for example, has been the focus of a number of studies that found that children co-operate more, display more returning behaviour, regulate themselves more, help others, show more empathy imaginativeness and creativity after watching the show Some evidence

---

[35] Friedrich & Stein, 1975

has forwarded that pro-social media efforts can cancel out the negative effects of violent content[36].

The research as pro-social uses of the media has focused on various aspects of children's growth. Potentially, children and to same degree adults can learn constructive social behaviour, for example, helpfulness, co-operation, friendliness, and imaginative play, from television viewing. It is less certain whether these positive benefits are actually being achieved[37].

Sacro and Silverman[38] offer five guiding principles necessary for successful media anticrime campaigns.

Firstly the information must be effectively disseminated, particularly in campaigns aimed at deterring crime.

Secondly, the relevance of campaign information must be gauged and the varying importance of crime to different segments of the public recognized.

---

[36] Heller& Polsky, 1976 p.290
[37] NTMH, 1982, Vol.1., p.90
[38] 1982

Thirdly, optimally no contradictions information concerning the danger of crime or the effectiveness of anticrime measures would be presented.

Fourthly, goals must be realistically defined to allow for both evaluation of the programme and efficient use of resources.

Lastly, to minimize the counter productive effects of heightening the salience of crime as a social issue by making the public believe that they are likely to be victimized, the campaign must clearly communicate what anticrime behaviour it is encouraging.

Media efforts to reduce victimization by teaching crime preventive behaviour have had mixed results. The expended capabilities of the media made possible by its technological advances have also affected how the media and report. Do. they increase the fear of crime, perpetuate or exacerbate the stereo types promoted by the entertainment media, and create support for or opposition to specific criminal justice policies is the question the has to be considered.

3.2.3 Women

Nearly all of television portrays attraction between men and women. It is part of human interaction. The problem is often times actors give us a skewed, unrealistic perception of how it happens between men and women when we watch it. The scary thing is we have all been at least a little conditioned through sitcoms, films, soap operas and even the not-so-real reality television. Most times people don't realize it.

Kelly McGillis watched that "I have always watched loads of television and movies, ever since I was little I was forming my thoughts on the world and relationships based on watching media. And for the most part, I think it was a hindrance for my game. Think about all those movies where the quiet, shy, yet uniquely cool guy pines after some gorgeous girl and after some conflict usually involving another douche bag, she comes around and they fall in love. Almost like a fairy tale. Because I could identify with 'that' guy, which I think a lot of guys can; I thought that if I just kept being him that it would just work out. But in real life it rarely ever ends this way. Unless that guy decides to learn about women, attraction, body language, he will enjoy the same level of success he always has.

This illustrates an important point about whatever you have in life. You cannot expect things to change for the better if you are not making an effort to change them. Being shy, quiet but uniquely cute is not an effective strategy to meet women. I wish it were! I would have had much more success throughout my teens and early 20s. But it's just not how it works in real life! Hoping and praying are all fine and good but if you truly want something, have to make it happen.

Another unrealistic thing I often observe in films is that I see in a lot movies that don't realistically portray the approaches. Often in film, when men go and approach women for whatever reason, the women's is already displaying receptive body language as if she is already into him. Don't get me wrong, occasionally this will happen granted you have near flawless body language and good looks. But for the rest of us, it doesn't happen this ideally. We have to display some value. We have to take advantage of our communication skills a bit more. James Bond movies are renowned for doing this. James will catch a beautiful women staring at him, he walks over to her and coyly whispers something sexual in her ear and from then on she is all over him. As I said before, it can happen like this, but rarely is does attraction happen so smoothly.

Although most are bad and don't represent reality, there are a couple movies that I feel do paint a more realistic picture. If you watch Wedding Crashers, Both Owen Wilson and Vince Vaughn use something as close to classic textbook game as I have ever seen on the big screen. In the beginning in particular watch how Vince Vaughn goes from

Demonstrating Value by done balloon tricks for the kids to dancing with his 'target' girl. To which then he isolates her and builds a sense of connection talking about the philosophy of connectedness to which then he takes it physical. All of this is of course is done in a hilarious way but it portrays what I think of as a more accurate, proactive depiction of attraction. Another great movie to see is Don Juan Demarco. Johnny Deep creates a marvelous, seductive character that truly sees the beauty in all women. When you watch this one, observe his usage of imagery in how he describes the world and more importantly how he describes it to women. It's excellent stuff. Another good one to check out is the most recent remake of Alfie featuring Jude Law. Law emanates a natural charisma in this movie that is believable and as you watch, gets him many women". Top Gun is another great movie to watch. Observe the sexual tension between Tom Cruise and Kelly McGillis.

In conclusion, there is nothing wrong with watching films and television even if they portray an inaccurate picture of how it happens in the real world. Just make sure to recognize IT ISN'T REAL, and for the most part doesn't represent reality. It's time we reprogram the way we think about attraction[39].

Hum Log observed that, the first soap for the middle class was aired for the first time, millions of viewers across India sat glued to their sets sharing the joys and heartbreaks of the characters

---

[39] www.televisioninfluenceonwomen.com

and identifying with their middle class attitude. This was the first serial which discussed issues of family planning, freedom of choice to find a life partner or job and the role of women in society. This was followed by other 'identifiable' serials like 'Buniyaad', and mythological serials like 'Ramayan' and 'Mahabharat'. The Indian audience was well and truly ensnared by the variety of serials on offer. Soaps had finally arrived in India.

Such was the psychological impact of mythologies like 'Mahabharat', that, people would hurry up with their morning chores and then sit glued to the television sets, some even offering incense and flowers to the godly' characters of Lord Krishna! For a nation fed on religion right from birth, these serials fed on the religious psychology of the viewers and soon the characters of Ram, Sita, Krishna had a hysterical mass following. People would touch their feet in public; such was the identification with their psyche!

With a population close to 400 million individual viewers, and a bouquet of channels offering an exhausting, unlimited and formula-tested soaps of 'holier-than-thou women with huge red bind is, streams of vermilion and imitation mangalsutras, as opposed to the vamps with over the top pan-caked makeup and a perpetual evil look in eyes, Indian soaps have been playing with the psychological emotions of the common Indian women who are the primary target for high drama and suspense and who tend to favour the positive or the negative vibes given out by these women characters.

With the advent of soap factories like Balaji Telefilms, women have started swearing by the characters of 'Tulsi' of Kunki Saas Bhi Kabhi Bahu Thi... (the title itself making no sense as the story seems to have gone haywire), or 'Parvati' of 'Kahani Ghar Ghar Ki'. Such is the craze for these women characters that advertisements for marriages have inserts like, 'the girl should be like Tulsi'! The message is strong and clear, today's mother-in-law wants a girl who would be completely traditional, protect the family values of her in- laws (does not matter if she is abused and berated by one and all — misunderstandings are always cleared after six episodes of glycerine tears and high family drama) and respect her in-laws no matter how scheming they are. This is just an example to show the extent of psychological play soap can have on the mindset of the viewers.

It would be a long debate to get into the 'positivity and negativity' of the women characters. Almost all serials are women-dominated, and if one leaves the saas-bahu (family drama) and moves to the more modern soaps, there have been some great ones, that have taken up bold themes, uncommon themes and worked on them. Soaps like 'Astitva- Ek Prem Kahani', dealing with a young man falling in love with a much older woman, or 'Jassi Jaisi Koi Nahin', where a common ordinary looking girl makes it to the top on basis of her merit, have been some milestones in influencing the youth. 'Jassi Jaisi Koi Nahin', has inspired common looking girls, with no glamour to back them , to stand for themselves and crate their own niche in society, definitely a very positive play of psychological interpretation of the human mind.

The fact remains that how much ever critics cry themselves hoarse over the portrayal of women and the one sided views presented (since men hardly play any role in decision making), the serials will go on. A dedicated audience sits glued to the sets and in order to reward this , Star Channel (India) came up with the 'Star Parivaar Awards' where viewers are given a choice to create their own family of choice. So much so that there was a best 'Star Atithi', who shared the limelight with the hallowed starcast. The awards bring forward the view that soaps are not just limited to the women who stay at home, but also women who are working and who unwind with their daily boost of late night serials.

Serials in India, claim to have the pulse of their viewers, Balaji Telefllms mainstay Ekta Kapoor is of the idea that her serials are the essence of Indian sense and sensibility and her characters and plots are normal people and normal incidents. Again there is no getting into a debate over this since the majority of viewers swear over the characters and their actions. One thing is for sure, it can be an eyesore for some, some can hate it, there may be hysterical debats over them, but soaps are here to stay. They have found their way and embedded themselves into the mindset of millions across the country. If nothing binds to strangers, a discussion on soaps have bring forth the most animated response. Style statements are being set, progressive or regressive attitudes (depending on how one views the serial) are being set, and emotions are running wild as characters drip tears or acid. The ball has started rolling. The Indian soapy affair has begun[40].

3.3 Socio Economic impact

Development directly influences changes in employment and income opportunities in communities. Such changes may be more or less temporary[41] or may constitute a permanent change in the employment and income profile of the community should the development project bring long-term job opportunities for community residents[42]. Assessing these types of changes is an important component of social impact analysis because growth in employment places additional demands on community services and resources. For example, a development that brings lower-wage jobs to a community may generate the need for different types of housing in the area. Changes in income also influence the social environment in a number of ways such as raising or lowering the average standard of living for residents.

Socio-economic impact assessment is also important for assessing changes in a community's social well-being that result from development.

---

[40] www.psychologicalimpactoftelevisionserialsinIndia.com
[41] e.g., construction projects, or seasonal employment
[42] e.g., establishment of a light industrial, manufacturing, or commercial establishment

This type of social change is more difficult to quantify than changes in the social environment because the assessment relies on the perceptions of current and new residents about how a proposed development may affect their quality of life.

Social impact assessment of this nature is important because it can help local officials, planners, developers and the public identify and address potential conflicts of interest that may accompany development. In addition to quality of life issues, it is important to assess how a proposed development may influence neighborhood cohesion or cultural differences among members of the community.

3.3.1. QUALITY OF LIFE

The attitudes community residents have towards development and the specific actions being proposed as well as their perceptions of community and personal well-being are important determinants of the social effects of a proposed action. Such attitudes are a reflection of the quality of life residents seek to enjoy and preserve, whether it be limiting growth in order to maintain the rural image of a small community; expanding the boundaries of the village; or providing a variety of housing choices to new, diverse residents and businesses. Changes in a community's social well-being can be determined by asking the individuals and representatives of groups or neighborhoods in the area to make explicit their perceptions and attitudes about the anticipated changes in the social environment.

It is important to bear in mind that while certain individuals or community groups may be active and forthcoming with input into the planning process, other community groups[43] that may be equally or even disproportionately affected by the proposed development may be less vocal in expressing concerns and interests. In situations where traditionally disempowered groups may be impacted by a development, it is important to make a concerted effort to involve them in the social impact assessment process.

Depending on the resources available to conduct the socio-economic impact assessment

---

[43] e.g., low income or minority groups

and the specific objectives of the analysis, some methods may be more appropriate than others. At any rate, a list of references is provided at the end of this chapter to guide further efforts in conducting a socio-economic impact assessment.

Finally, it is important to note that a socio-economic impact assessment not only forecasts impacts, but should also identify means to mitigate adverse impacts. Mitigation should include efforts to avoid an impact by not taking or modifying an action; minimizing, rectifying or reducing the impacts through the design or operation of the project or policy; or compensating for the impact by providing substitute facilities, resources or opportunities[44].

UNIT – IV
Indian Constitution, other legislations and Judicial perspective

---

[44] www.socioeconomicimpactinIndia.com

4.1 Indian Constitution

The expression "freedom of the Press" has been understood in various senses. It is also confused with the idea of the independence of the press. The expression should be understood as meaning freedom to hold opinions, to receive and impart information through the printed word, without any interference from any public authority. The Indian Press Commission observed thus the freedom of the media while examining the "freedom of the press" and repeal or amendment of laws not in consonance with it.

The Constitution of India is the supreme law of the land. It is also a charter of Indian social, political, economic and cultural values. It epitomizes the people's hopes and aspirations. Freedom of speech and expression is protected by Article 19 (1) (a) of the Indian Constitution. This freedom provides the platform for one to freely express opinions or convictions by speaking, writing, printing pictures, or in any other manner. The courts with regard to its nature, scope and extent of this fundamental right have not exhaustively commented upon this freedom guaranteeing all citizens freedom of speech and expression. Freedom of speech and expression is the foundation of democracy.

Media freedom is fundamental for free public discussion, education and health, to the life of an individual in a democratic polity. The media is one of the vital pillars of an free society. The right to freedom of speech and expression extend to communication media sections. Its effect on state owned television is little influenced.

This freedom does not confer any absolute right to speak or disseminate without responsibility whatever one wishes. It also does not provide unrestricted or unbridled immunity for every possible use of language and prevent the punishment of those who abuse this freedom. The Constitution of the United States of America says in the amendment "Congress shall make no law abridging the freedom of speech".

The Constitution of India guarantees various civil rights to the citizens of this country. The Article 19[45] provides the common law rights and are recognized and guaranteed as the natural rights and are fundamental in nature. The effect is that the rights can only be restricted but not abrogated. A limitation on the exercise of the right of freedom of speech and expression to be valid it must be imposed by a valid law and the restriction imposed by executive action will be invalid. The restrictions should be reasonable and proximately related to the purposes mentioned in Article 19 (2)[46].

Article 19 (1) (a) provides "that all the citizens shall have the right to freedom of speech and expression". Although Article 19 (1) (a) does not mention the freedom of the press it was early settled by judicial decisions that freedom of speech and expression includes freedom of the press and circulation. Also it excludes to the freedom of television.

4.2 Judicial Perspective

[45] Seervai, H.M, constitutional law of India, 1982, PP192-195.
[46] Shukla K.C, Constitution of India, Asian Law House. 1988, P.P. 250 – 252.

Ramesh Vs. Union of India[47], the court considered whether the televising of a TV serial "Tamas", depicting communal violence during the pre-partition period, was violative of Section 5-B of the Cinematograph Act, 1952. The Supreme Court held that the unanimous approval of the examining body must given full weight, especially when was supported by a further examination by the TV authorities from the viewpoint of public acceptability and was also approved by a Division Bench of the Bombay High Court. In dismissing the challenge, the Supreme Court again emphasised that:

"The potency of the motion picture is as much for good as for evil. If some scenes of violence, some nuances expression or some events in the film can stir up certain feelings in the spectator, an equally deep, strong, lasting and beneficial impression can be conveyed by scenes revealing the machinations of selfish interests, scenes depicting mutual respect and tolerance, scenes showing comradeship, help and kindness which transcend the barriers of religion. What is necessary sometimes is to penetrate behind the

---

[47] 1988 (1) SCC 668

scenes and analyze the causes of such conflicts. The attempt the author in this film is to draw a lesson from our country's past history, expose the motive of persons who operate behind the scenes to generate and foment conflicts and to emphasis the desire of persons to live in amity and the need for them to rise above religious barriers and treat one another with kindness, sympathy and affection. It is possible only for a motion picture conveys such a message in depth and if it is able to do this, it will be an achievement of great social value."

In judging the likely effect of the exhibition of a film or of reading a book, the court relied on the famous passage from Justice Vivian Bose in B.C Shukla Vs. Provincial Government[48] which said the standard must be of reasonable, strong-minded, firm and courageous men or as has been said in English Law, "the man on the top of a Clapham omnibus", and not those of weak and vacillating minds nor of those who scent danger in every hostile point of view.

---

48 AIR 1947 Nag I

Odyssey Communications Pvt. Ltd. Vs. Lokvidyan Svnghatana (1983.3 SCC 410), the apex court made explicit that a citizen's right to show films on TV is part of the fundamental right under Article 19(l)(a) which can be curtailed only under circumstances set out in Article 19(2) and not otherwise. Accordingly, an interim injunction restraining the TV serial "Honi Anhony" for spreading false and superstitious beliefs was vacated.

The Tamil film, "Ore Oru Gramathule" (In One Village), had its "U" certificate revoked by a Divisional Bench of the Madras High Court, for "irresponsibly" criticising the caste-based reservation policy of the State Government and suggesting its replacement by economic based reservations, which would lead to a volatile public reaction. In the Supreme Court, (S. Rangarajan Vs. P Jagjivan Ram (1989) 2 SCC 574), Justice Jagannatha Shetty noted that the film was approved by two revising committees for grant of "U" certificate; that an opinion on the certifiability of a film must focus on the main theme and not on isolated passages in the film; that a film maker is entitled to project his own message which others may disapprove of; that the board or court should not hesitate to approve a him criticising government policies, if it is otherwise unobjectionable and constitutionally permissible, merely because of threats of violence by some disgruntled persons and accordingly reversed the decision of the High Court.

LIC Vs. Manubhai Shah[49], the petitioner's award winning documentary film on the Rhopal Gas tragedy, titled, "Beyond Genocide", was awarded a "U" certificate by the Censors but was refused to be telecast by Doordarshan for being "outdated", "irrelevant", imbalanced, critical of State Government rehabilitation and that compensation claims of victims were sub-judice. The Supreme Court held that Doordarshan, being a State controlled agency financed by public funds, was not justified in refusing to telecast the film and that once the censors had awarded a "U" certificate, Doordarshan cannot refuse to exhibit it.

4.3 Other Legislations

---

49 1992. (3) SCC 637

The Official Secrets Act, 1923 (Act XIX of 1923) has been passed to consolidate and amend the law relating to official secrets. This Act contains only fifteen sections and is of a general nature and has had a great impact on the press. The act is aimed at maintaining security of the State against leakage of secret information, sabotage and the like. It deals with two kinds of offences, namely spying[50] and wrongful communication[51] of secret information. It fixes penal liability for wrongful communication on all persons who are in way any involved, either directly or indirectly in transmitting or receiving wrongful communication of secret information.

Section 5 of the Act gives the executive power to prosecute any one disclosing official information, or any person voluntarily receiving such information[52].

In Nandlal More V. state[53], the Punjab High Court held that the budget proposals are secret documents, because their premature disclosure is

[50] Section 3
[51] Section 5
[52] Section 5 (2)
[53] 1965 (1) Cr. Li. 392 (Punj)

not in the public interest and might cause an individual to dump goods or speculate on the stock exchange.

S.P. Gupta V. President of India[54], the Supreme Court

Took a liberal view of the disclosure of official documents under section 123 of the Indian Evidence Act, 1872 and held that the court had a right to inspect secret documents in order to decide whether they are related to affairs of the state and on balance public interest justified their disclosure. It rejected the theory of "class documents".

The Act is aimed at prohibiting the production in India of crime and violent publications. Pictorial and other publications containing stories of glorification of crime, violence are in circulation in large number. The dissemination of such stories is likely to encourage antisocial tendencies among children and exert a harmful influence on young persons. The Young Persons (Harmful Publications) Act,

---

[54] A.I.R 1982 s.C. 149

1956 has been passed to prevent the disaffection of certain publications harmful to young persons.

Harmful publications are dealt with-in section 2 of the Act. It means any book, magazine, pamphlet, leaflet, newspaper or other publication which consist of stories with the aid of picture or without the aid of pictures or wholly in pictures being stories portraying wholly or mainly.

(I) the commission of offences or (ii) acts of violence or cruelty or (iii) incidents of repulsive or horrible nature.

The government has power to declare harmful publications to be forfeited. It shall be lawful for army police officer to seize the harmful publication. The Act also gives power (section 6) to seize and destroy harmful publication. The publications are empowered to seize any publication found in a suspected place.

The Cinematograph Act of 1918 dealt generally with the examination and certification of films as suitable for public exhibition and regulation of cinemas including their licensing. Cinema is a concern of both the central and state governments. The Cinematography Act, 1952 has been passed to make provisions for a certification of cinematograph films for exhibition and for regulating exhibitions by means of cinematograph.

The official examination of film before public exhibition is censorship. The Censor Board has power to remove any of the contents of the film which are thought to be indecent, obscene or which might offend people. The word censorious means looking for mistakes or faults in the film; censorship is a process of censor or censoring. The law insists that no film should be exhibited publicly unless it is first submitted to a Central Board of Film Censors and it is approved.

The Ministry of Information and Broadcasting has simplified and nationalized the film censorship directions and issued fresh guidelines in the form directions in clearing films for public exhibition. The revised gave greater scope to the serious minded and sensitive creators of aesthetic films and ensure that restrictions on artist expression are truly reasonable and reflective only of the requirements of the law. The guidelines have been evolved after taking note of the recommendations of the Enquiry Committee on Film Censorship and the views expressed by the film industry.

Some of the objectives of film censorship are

(a) The medium of film remains responsible and sensitive to the values and standards of society.

(b) Artistic expression and creative freedom are not unduly curbed, and

(c) Censorship is responsible to social change. In pursuance of the above objectives

(I) Anti-social activities such as violence are not glorified or justified.

(ii) The modus operandi of criminals or other visuals or words likely to invite the commission are not depicted.

(iii) Pointless or avoidable scenes of violence, cruelty and horror are not shown

(iv) Human sensibilities are not offended by vulgarity, obscenity and depravity;

(v) Visuals or words contemptuous of racial religious or other groups are not presented.

Films that meet the above-mentioned criteria but are considered unsuitable for exhibition to non-adults shall be certified for exhibition of adult audience only.

The Cinematograph Act has been amended with a view to discouraging the exhibition of uncertified films. The Cinematograph Amendment Act 1984, which came into force on 27 August 1984 provides in section 7 for enhanced punishment for the exhibition of uncertified film, including video film. A minimum punishment has also been prescribed for offences relating to the exhibition of uncertified video films.

The Act penalizes the abuse of the freedom of the press by publication of matter involving encouragement of violence or sabotage or incitement to certain other many grave offences. Objectionable matter was defined to mean any words, sign, or visible representation[55].

The objectionable matter as defined in the act include anything bringing hatred or contempt, or excite disaffection towards the Government established by law in India or in any state thereof and thereby cause or tend to cause public disorder. Anything which invite any person to

---

[55] Section3

interfere with the production, supply or distribution of food, or anything which causes fear or alarm to the public or to any section of the public whereby any person may be induced to commit an offence against the state or against the public tranquility.

The Act further defines objectionable matter as something which invites any person or any class or community of persons to committee murders, mischief or any other offence, visual presentations which are grossly indecent or secular or obscene or intended for blackmail.

The Government by lawful means remove matter which are producing or have a tendency to produce disharmony. In considering whether any matter is objectionable matter under this Act, the effect of the words, signs or visible representations, and not the intention of keeper of the press or publisher or editor shall be taken into account.

The protection from annexation and infringement by others of the fruits of an authors labour, skill or intellect, through the creation of a proprietary and statutory right that he acquires in his work, is the primary aim of the enactment of the Copyright Act, 1957.

The author shall be the first owner of the copyright subject to the provisions of section 17 of the Act, and he will have the sole right to produce the work in any material form he likes. The Copyright (Amendment) Act of 1983 and the Copyright (Amendment) Act of 1984 have extensively amended the Act of 1957, seeking to include within its purview the modern media of communication, such as video films, duplications equipment, compilations, computer programmes, etc and to make punishment for infringement of copyright law.

Infringement of copyright is a trespass on a private domain owned and occupied by the owner of the copyright and therefore punishable by law. A copyright is deemed to be infringed only when an act is done without the consent of owner of the copyright. Section 52 enumerates the acts "that wouldn't constitute infringement of copyright, since such acts are arguably done in the public interest", as was held in Blackwood and Sons Ltd., V.A.Parasuraman[56].

Protection against infringement is not infinite. Since the infringement of copyright is not only a civil but also a criminal wrong, the Act provides for both civil and criminal action in the case of an encroachment of the copyright of the owner. The civil remedies for infringement of copyright are provided in section 54 to 62 of the copyright Act 1957. In R. G.Anand V.Delux films[57] the Supreme Court said that since a violation of copyright amounts to an act of piracy, it must be proved by clear and cogent evidence.

Provisions of the Indian Penal Code:

The Indian Penal Code contain certain provision which prevent sale of obscene books and objects to young person etc.,

For the purpose of section 292 a book, pamphlet, paper, writing, drawing, painting, representation, figure or any other object, shall be deemed to be obscene if it is lascivious or appeals to the prurient interest of its effect, or the effect of any one of its items, is, if taken as a whole, such

---

[56] AIR. 1949 Mad 410
[57] A.I.R 1978 S.C. 1913

as to tend to deprave and corrupt persons who are likely, having regard to all relevant circumstances, to read, see or hear the matter contained or embodied in it.

The section makes provision for punishment on first conviction with imprisomiient of either description for a term which may extend to two years and fine and in the event of second or subsequent conviction, with imprisonment of either description for a term which may extend to five years, and also with five which may extend to five thousand rupees sale etc., of obscene objects to farms person. Under Sec.293, whoever sells, lets to hire, distributed, exhibits or circulates to any person under the age of twenty years any such obscene object as is referred to in the last preceding section, or offers or attempts to do so, shall be punished on first conviction with imprisonment of either description for a term which may extend to three years, and with fine which may extend to two thousand rupees, and, in the event of a second or subsequent conviction, with imprisonment of either description for a term which may extend to seven years, and also with fine which may extend to five thousand rupees.

UNIT – V
Conclusion and suggestions

The main thrust of the study was to find out the effects of television watching by people and its socio-legal consequences. The impact of television watching was seen with regard to violence, sex, crudity, depicted in television shows and its adverse impact on society: adults, women and children. Attempts were also made to find out the extent to which exposure to satellite television programmes had created a change in the cultural, social and ethical values. The awareness of legal consequences among the viewers also been solicited. The historical background of the advent of television and its consequential growth is being observed. The freedom of the press; whether it can be extendable to television and the constitutional and legislative procedure are presented for a clear understanding of the study.

The aim of the Constitution framers was that the freedom of speech and expression to be guaranteed with certain restrictions. Such freedom was actionable in the event of misuse of that freedom. The freedom is guaranteed as a fundamental right though the word freedom of the press/media is not specifically mentioned. The guaranteeing of the freedom of the press by the United States constitution has saw a surge in the growth of television industry. The right enabled the programme makers to provide uninhibited access to information. It also provided a platform, which has made the television industry show the world its might. The growth of television also bought several changes in the society.

The freedom of the press forms part of the democratic values enshrined in the constitution. The extension of this right to electronic media has revolutionized the thought process of ordinary Indian. It exposed him to the New World order of which he was not so familiar. The reasonable restrictions imposed under Article 19-clause (2) has made the television viewing somewhat decent.

From the first Amendment to the constitution of India, which was the result of a judicial decision[58] has followed the liberalization of the reasonable restrictions imposed on the freedom of the press/media. The fourth estate having a bearing effect on the other estates has

---

[58] Ramesh Vs Union of India 1988, 1SCC 668

become a determining factor in deciding the nature regime that should exist. Past political developments and the role the press/media played during emergency and the role played by a vernacular paper/television in the change of guard in Andhra Pradesh indicates its strength.

People today live in two worlds; a real world and a media world. The first in limited by direct experience; the second is bounded only by the decisions of editors and producers to what extent the media actually influence people's attitudes, and how significantly, have been the subject of some argument. Those ascertaining that the media significantly affect people's attitudes about crime commonly argue that the vast majority of our exposure to crime and violence comes from the media public surveys have reported that as many as 95 percent of the general population cite the media as their primary source of information about crime.

The television is the cheapest and most popular form of amusement. No other means of mass media has such a profound impact and entertainment standards compared to the cinema. The impact of television on the society derives from two of its very important characteristics. Its popularity as a cheep and easily available means of entertainment and secondary its audio-visual appeals to the mind. The television can develop into a very powerful weapon to educate the masses or to change their mind properly guided, the television might have a healthy influence on national life and character.

Television can amuse people in different ways. The ordinary family is escaping the hard realities of life with the illusion created by television. The television is making us witness the live phenomena. More than any other medium television threatens parent's control over their children's received view of the world. The cognitive accessibility of the message inherent in its audio-visual symbol system makes this increasingly possible. Researcher also suspect that television use greatly reduced both comic book reading and cinema attendance, had a lesser effect on the use of print fiction, and had very little impact on non fiction reading.

The reality of the media depicts with regard to crime and justice is opposite to any objective measure of reality. Violence constitutes a significant portion of the total news. The lack reality information in the media further mystifies and obscures criminality. The media emphasize individual personality traits on the cause of crime and violent interdiction as its solution. The media also appear to subtly but significantly affect attitudes about crime and violence. These media effects interact with other factors, are difficult to discuss, and are difficult to counteract.

In general, television portrayals of crime and justice appear to influence most easily children's and women factual perceptions, such as the amount of crime they believe to be occurring, and to have less direct influence on overall evaluations of social conditions or ideas about what should be done.

The evidence of an increase is social aggression following expose to violent visual media content is clear in the survey but it may be mixed in the society. The research suggests, without conclusively powering, that the influence of television on the society and its consequential aggressiveness is high because of the mass media communication of television. The television influence on criminality, independent of its effect, as aggressive behaviour has not adequately been directly explored. The study suggests that media may very well affect crime independently of violent content.

The research shows that the television content affects adults, women and children's beliefs, attitudes, and knowledge on a variety of other issues and topics, including occupational knowledge and expectations. It is important to note that mass media effects on adults, women and children do not occur in a vacuum. Media are only one of many contributions to the adults, women and children's beliefs about and behaviour in the world.

The media have increased their capability to discover and deliver information about the world, the television has moved instead toward greater reliance on created, pre-packaged information, stereo types, and entertainment — style content. As a result, the people receive an image of crime that not only is unnecessarily distorted but supports basically one approach to anti crime policy. The research reveals that commercialization is forcing the media to perpetrate its image. They continue to produce versions of what has been produced and found acceptable in past.

In determining what is socially acceptable with regard to crime and violence that cultural forces come into play. As a culture, we embrace the crime and justice images that the media portray. Depictions of criminals and perpetrators both entertain and comfort children. They entertain because they scare and comfort because they relieve. In a society with pervasive, multimedia, mass media systems, the public is more tolerant of surveillance. Evidence is building that the media alter reality by affecting ways in which the audience perceives, interprets, and behaves toward it.

To solve and prevent crimes the government must interview in its citizen's lives. The television provides a means to do so in new ways, ways that are considered both more efficient and less obviously intrusive.

A new set of guiding principles regarding the media's influences on public attitudes emerged
(1) The mass media may help form attitudes toward new subjects where little prior opinion exists.

(2) The mass media may influence attitudes that are weakly held.

(3) The mass media may strengthen one attitude at the expense of a series of others when the strength of the several attitudes in evenly balanced.

(4) The mass media can change even strongly held attitudes when they are able to report new facts.

(5) The mass media may suggest new courses of action that appear to better satisfy wants and needs.

(6) The mass media's strongest and most universally recognized effect remains the reinforcement or strengthening of predisposition.

Besides noting the media's potential usefulness and effects, these principles also highlight the difficulty of using the mass media effectively and the limited scope within which they can be used. Because of the multiple paths and complex social networks lying between the public and the media, it is also generally accepted that the media's influence can reach even those that do not watch, read, or listen

It is clearly evident from the study that the television is encroaching upon the values of the society. The impact on children has become a major contribution for the erosion of values in the society as the ideology of a society is shaped when the mind is young. The advent of Internet has made the children struck their heads into the computer and explores the wide network to get a glimpse of nakedness.

Television does influence the life style of the children. Their education is severely suffered and there is an impact on health also. Children are spending hours together before the television set ignoring education, sports, and cultural activity. The viewing time is more during the vacations and holidays.

To control the evil effects of television a number of measures have to be undertaken. The government, the society, and the family play a vital role in this. The legal regulation has opened up the skies for free flow material without any firewall. In the name of the "Freedom of the media" the television has eroded many legal norms. The commercialization of this industry has made to work for personal benefit at the cost of the society. Various laws enacted for purpose of controlling the media have failed in achieving their objectives.

The legal regulation has become a paper tiger under which the government tries to protect itself the media glare has overshadowed the legal regulation. This is resulted in the non-implementations of various laws. The technology innovation has made the television media grow into out of proportion from the clutches of law. The age-old laws have become obsolete and they are not helping the law enforcing authorities in curbing the violation of regulation. The tendency has to be curbed by making stringent laws. The laws are to be amended so as to be able to punish the abuse of "freedom of media".

- There shall be a provision for pre-censorship of television programmes. not all the programmes, those having inflammatory content shall be restricted before it being aired freely. To achieve this is a regulation to pre-censorship of objectionable programmes has to be established.
- The government should develop. It's technology to control the waves of foreign

media. Highly sophisticated equipment of foreign channels directly/ telecasting programmes into the drawing rooms. These channels are offering a wide variety content on which the local laws are not in a position to exercise control. The stuff telecast by channels like 'Fashion TV" have caused furor all over the countries. The government was forced to announce the banning of this channel despite that the channels are aired on television as there is no mechanisms with the government to stop it.

- The present laws are not adequate to curb telecasting of such channels. The provisions contained in them are not adequate to implement the policy decisions. There is an urgent need to enact laws, which can practically curb the menace of foul channels telecasting violence, sex, obscenity, crudity in the form of fashion, modem culture. Such laws should be strongest to provide penal provisions, which can deter the occurrence of such activity. Imposing fines for violation should regulate the cable operations and Internet service provides.

- The children are the greatest assets of a nation. By allowing a vulnerable class to exposure of unhealthy medium, which could spoil their future, the gravest error is being committed.

The advent of Internet has further opened the floodgates for the unethical media. It introduced pornography into the entertainment viewing of children. The children are falling pray to such web sites, which offer a kaleidoscope of material, which is not acceptable in army standard in any of nation.

The researcher suggests that a National Commission for Children shall be established as a constitutional body. This commission has to work for the overall development of child. Its aim shall be that every child should grow as a responsible citizen. The exploitation of children has to be controlled by this authority.

More educational programmes are to be produced for children. Instead of what is being produced now by the government departments and independent bodies, such programmes should be inn6vative. The research has shown that adults, women and children prefer entertainment and infotainment more to educational programmes. Hence it .Has become imperative, in order to attract this audience group those qualities imbibed in educational programmes

Then Extra-curricular activity of children should also be developed. They should be encouraged to participate in social-functions, sports and social service. The research indicates that are spending the vacations and holiday watching television. To avoid such a situation they should be sent to excursions and tours, which provide an insight into the real world.

The myth created by television is often confused with reality and this veil should be lifted to provide the real picture.

The researcher sums up the study with an optimistic note that television has grown from an entertainment medium into an influential factor. The significance of this media is that it can lead to the development of a distinct portrayal for children. The trend toward separate realms of information that was accessible only to a select group is also spreading to all. Its influence and children and its easy accessibility could be a shot in the arm to conquer the world. There is a need for further exploration of this field having socio-legal consequence. The social influence of this media will be ever increasing as the clutches of law always falling short of apprehending this force. A proper balance between the media and law is the need of the day.

Especially to control the obscene programmes telecasting in certain channels coming from other countries an international moral code should be established.

BIBLIOGRAPHY

Amarjit Mahajan , Nirupama Luthra Family and Television, Gyan Publishing House. New Delhi 1993.

Ambedkar's draft, article II(l)(12) and (7) select documents 11 4(u) (d) Austrialian Press Council (Annual Report No.2), 1981 A.I.R 130,134

Andyson, F. 1977, TV violence and viewer aggression ,Public Opinion Quarterly 41

Bandura, A (1968) "What Tv Violence can Do to You Child". In Violence and Mass Media, New York, Harper & Row

Bandura, A. (1973). Aggression: A social learning analysis. Englewood Cliffs, NJ: Prentice Hall.

Bandura, A. (1978). Social learning theory of aggression" Journal of of Communication. 28(3)

Berkowitz, L (1963) "Film violence and subsequent aggressive tendencies" Public Opinion Quarterly - 27

Berkowitz, L. (1984) "Some effect of thoughts on Anti- and prosocial influences of Media Events. Psychological bulletin 95.

Bhaskar Rao, Raghavan Social Effect of Mass Media in India.

Chombart, delauwe & Marie Jose (1985). "Child and TV interaction" Centre national recherche scientifique. Paris

Churchill, Roberts (1981). "Children's & Parents TV viewing and Perceptions of violence"

Clor, Obscenity And The Public Morality, (1969) p.146

Comstock G. (1980). Television in America Beverly Hills. Sage Publication.

Comstock G. (1983). Media influences on Aggression, in Prevention in control of Aggression. NY, Pergamon Press

Constitution of India, 1950

Dexter & White People, society, and Mass Communications, the free,, Press NY

Dorr, Annie(1986). Television and Children: A special medium for

Education.

Encyclopedia Americana, 1976

George Gerbner, Mass Media policies in changing cultures.

Gopal Saxena, Television in India Changes and ChaHenges.

Graber ,D. (1980) Crime News and the Public New York: Praeger

Greenberg,B (1969) "The content and Context of Violence in the Media"

Howe, Michael (1977). Television and Children, London New University

Indirect Effects on Aggression against Women". Journal of Social issues 42.

Jagadish Swamp Constitution of India 1984

Larson, D.N. (1968). Violence and Mass Media. NewYork. Harper & Row.

Malamuth , N. & Briere ,J (1986) "Sexual Violence in the Media:

Mc Grawhill Encyclopedia of Science and Technology Vol.13, Television /

Munshi's draft, article V (1) and (2) select documents II, 4
(ii) (b) p.75

New Standard Encyclopedia

O'keefe.G(1984) "Public Views on Crime Television
Exposure and Media credibility, New bury park,
calif: Sage

Patriot, 3rd June, 1995.

Pandy J.N, constitutional Law of India, Asian Law house,
2008.

Payne Fund Studies 1984.

Pourtois, Jean Pierre (1978). "Does TV violence affect
aggressive behaviour in children? Cited in
Sociological Abstract 1984.

Sacco.V & Silverman (1982) Crime prevention through
Mass Media Prospects and Problems.

Seervai H.M, Constitution law of India, Asian law house,
1982.

ShivaRao, B. Framing of India's Constitution

Singh D.K. Constitutional law of India.

Special Audience. Beverly Hill, Sage Publications.

Surette, Ray, Media Crime & Criminal Justice 1992, Brooks/Cole Pacific,,,' Grove, California

Sukla K.C, Constitution of India, 1988.

The New Encyclopedia Britanica, 1987

The Obscenity laws : a report by the working party 1969.

Yadava J.S. & U.V. Reddi (1988). "In the midst of diversity: TV in Urban Indian Homes". InJames Lull(ed) World Families Television, Beverly Hills, Sage Publications.

Zucker, H: 1978 "The Variable Nature of News Media influence". In Communication Yearbook Vol.2

List of Websites :

www.indiantelevision.com/

www.wikipedia.org/wiki/Television-in-india

www.Documents and setting / sarada / Desktop / psychological impact of television serials. 3/2/2009.

www.indianchild .com/ India – television.

www.impact of television on adults

www. impact of television on women and children.

www.impact of economics in India

LIST OF CASES

A.K. Gopalan Vs. The state of Madras (1950) S.C.J 174

Associated Press Vs. U.S. (1945) 325 U.S.

B.C. Shukla Vs. Provincial Government A.I.R. 1947 Nag (1).

Blackwood and Sons Ltd Vs. A. Parasuraman A.I.R. 1949 Mad 410

Brij Bushan Vs. State of Delhi, 1950, S.C.R. 605

Express Newspapers Private Limited Vs. Union of India 1958 S.C.578

Gitlow Vs. New York, 69 ,L ed 1138

K.A. Abbas Vs. Union of India A.I.R. (1971) S.C. 481

LIC Vs. Manubhai Shah. 1992 (3), SCC 637.

Lovell Vs. Griffin (1938) 303 U.S.

M.S.M. Sharma Vs. Shri Krishna sinha (1959) supp.1 S.C.R. 806.

Nandlal More Vs. State, 1965 (1) Cri L.J. 392 (Punj)

Odyssey Communications Pvt., Ltd., Vs. Lokvidyan Svnghatana. 1983 (3) SCC 410.

Rangarajan Vs. P. Jagjivan Ram. 1989 (2) SCC 574.

R.G. Anand Vs. Delux Films A.I.R 1978 S.C. 1913.

Raj Kapoor Vs. Delhi Administration A.I.R. 1980 S.C. 258.

Rajit D. Udeshi Vs. State of Mahashtra A.I.R 1965 S.C. 881

Ramesh Vs.Union of India, 1988 (1) SCC 668.

Re Bharati Press Case, A.I.R. 1951, Patna, 12.

Re Hindu Case A.I.R. 1980 p.101

Re Staternan's Case (1967) A.R. 45

Rex Vs. Hicklin (1868) 3QB360

Romesh Thaper Vs. State of Modras, A.I.R. 1950, S.c. 124.

S.P. Gupta Vs. President of India A.I.R. 1982 S.C. 149

Schnerden Vs. Irwington (1939) 308 U.S.)

Stanley Vs. Georgia 394 U.S. 557

State of Bihar Vs. Shailabala Devi 1952 S.C.J. 465.

State of Bihar Vs. Shailabala Devi A.I.R. 1952 S.C. 329

Sukanta Haider Vs. The State A.I.R. 1952 Cal 214

Thomas Vs. collins (1945) 322 U.S.

www.ingramcontent.com/pod-product-compliance
Lightning Source LLC
Chambersburg PA
CBHW070817180526
45168CB00002B/646